The Fenians

Photographs and memorabilia from the National Museum of Ireland

Michael Kenny

Country House, Dublin
in association with
The National Museum of Ireland

Published in 1994 by
Town House and Country House
42 Morehampton Road
Donnybrook
Dublin 4
Ireland

in association with The National Museum of Ireland

British Library Cataloguing in Publication Data. A catalogue record for this book is available from the British Library.

ISBN: 0-946172-42-0

Acknowledgements
The author and publishers would like to thank the National Library of Ireland for permission to reproduce Photos 22 and 27.
   Special thanks to Valerie Dowling for photography, to Joseph Aylward, Catherine McIvor, Rosaline Murphy and Margaret O'Shaughnessy of the National Museum for their assistance, and to Oliver Snoddy for help and advice.
   The kind assistance of the Ancient Order of Hibernians and Clan na Gael in the United States is also gratefully acknowledged.

Design: Bill Murphy
Colour origination: The Kulor Centre
Printed in Ireland by Criterion Press, Dublin

CONTENTS

THE BACKGROUND

In 1798 the United Irishmen, a secret revolutionary organisation, rose in rebellion, seeking an end to British rule in Ireland and the establishment of an independent republic. The rebellion was suppressed with great brutality, but the principles of the movement were to have a profound influence on the course of Irish history. Its stated aim 'to break the connection with England, the never failing source of all our political evils . . . and to substitute the common name of Irishmen in place of the denomination of Protestant, Catholic and Dissenter' was to inspire later generations of republicans.

Following the collapse of the rebellion, the British prime minister William Pitt introduced a bill to abolish the Irish parliament and effect a Union between Ireland and Britain. Opposition from the Protestant oligarchy that controlled the parliament was countered by the widespread and open use of bribery. The Act of Union was passed, and became law on 1 January 1801. The Catholic majority, who were excluded from the Irish parliament, were promised emancipation under the Union. The promise was not kept, however, and the early decades of the new century witnessed a protracted and bitter struggle for Catholic civil liberties. The British government reluctantly conceded emancipation in 1829, but simultaneously disenfranchised the small tenants, known as 'forty shilling freeholders', who were largely Catholics. For these, the ground troops of the emancipation struggle, the victory proved a rather hollow one.

Daniel O'Connell, who had led the emancipation crusade, utilised the same peaceful constitutional methods in his next campaign, to have the Act of Union with Britain repealed. Petitions, monster meetings and huge displays of popular support were insufficient, however, against a government for whom the Union was infinitely more important than Irish public opinion. O'Connell failed and his failure had a major influence on the thinking of those who attempted armed rebellion in 1848, 1849 and 1867.

In the early 1840s the younger radicals in the repeal movement, impatient with O'Connell's over-cautious policies, formed what became known as the Young Ireland movement. In 1842 three of the Young Ireland leaders, Thomas Davis, Charles Gavan Duffy and John Blake Dillon, launched the *Nation* newspaper. Stirred by the writings of Davis and imbued with the romantic nationalism of the time, a generation of idealists set out to create a spirit of self-respect and an identity based on nationality rather than on social status or religion. Following the virtual collapse of the repeal movement and the onset of famine, the Young Irelanders broke away completely from O'Connell in 1846. O'Connell himself died the following year.

Photo 1. Thomas Davis (1814–45). Born at Mallow, Co Cork, he became leader of the Young Ireland movement and launched the Nation *newspaper in 1842. Author of the famous ballads 'A Nation Once Again' and 'The West's Asleep'. He died of fever at thirty-one years of age.*

1.

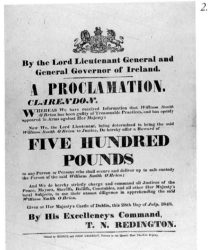

2.

Photo 2. Reward of five hundred pounds for the capture of William Smith O'Brien, 1848.

The blight that destroyed the potato harvest between 1845 and 1849 caused a human tragedy of unprecedented proportions. An entire social class of smallholders and labourers, totally dependent on the crop and lacking the cash with which to purchase alternative food, was virtually wiped out by hunger, disease and emigration. The *laissez-faire* economic thinking of the day also ensured that government help was slow, reluctant and insufficient. Between 1845 and 1851 the population fell by almost two million. The enduring folk memory of a people starving while livestock and grain continued to be exported, often under military guard, left a legacy of bitterness and resentment among the survivors. The great exodus of the famine and post-famine years also ensured that such feelings were not confined to Ireland, but spread to England, the United States, Australia and other countries where Irish emigrants gathered.

Shocked by the horrors of starvation and influenced by the revolutions then sweeping Europe, the Young Irelanders moved from agitation to armed rebellion in 1848. The attempt failed utterly, after a minor skirmish at Ballingarry, Co Tipperary, and a few lesser incidents. The reasons were three-fold — inadequacy of military preparations, lack of unity of purpose among the leaders, and the total despondence of the people after three years

3.
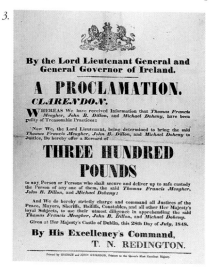

4.

Photo 3. Reward of three hundred pounds for the capture of Thomas Francis Meagher, John Blake Dillon and Michael Doheny, 1848.

Photo 4. John Mitchel (1815–75). A prominent Young Irelander born at Dungiven, Co Derry. Sentenced to fourteen years' transportation in 1848, and escaped in 1853. His Jail Journal *has been described as a classic of prison literature. Returned to Ireland 1874 and elected MP for Tipperary.*

of famine. The leaders fled, their followers dispersed. A last flicker of revolt in 1849 was equally unsuccessful.

John Mitchel, the most committed advocate of revolution, had been arrested early in 1848 and transported to Australia. He was soon joined by other leaders, such as William Smith O'Brien and Thomas Francis Meagher who had been rounded up after Ballingarry. John Blake Dillon escaped to France, as did three of the younger leaders, James Stephens, John O'Mahony and Michael Doheny. Most of them made their way from

Photo 5. James Stephens (1825–1901). Born in Kilkenny city, he worked as a civil engineer before being wounded at Ballingarry in 1848. He escaped to France, returning in the 1850s to found and organise the IRB. He was replaced after the failures of 1865–66, and spent much of his remaining life in Paris.

Photo 6. John O'Mahony (1816–77). Born near Kilbeheny, Co Limerick, he took part in the 1848 rebellion, after which he escaped via France to America. Founder of the Fenian Brotherhood, he devoted his life to furthering its aims. A fine classical and Gaelic scholar, he died penniless in a New York tenement.

France to the United States, where they were joined by Meagher and Mitchel, both of whom escaped from Australia. It was these younger refugees and escapees who were to provide the leadership for the two republican organisations set up at the end of the 1850s, one in Ireland, the other in America.

The republican movement in Ireland was known as the Irish Republican Brotherhood (IRB), and its American equivalent was named the Fenian Brotherhood. Both bodies were to find their greatest support among the displaced survivors of the famine. Members of both groups and indeed sympathisers who were not in either organisation were commonly termed 'Fenians' by the contemporary media and commentators.

THE IRISH REPUBLICAN BROTHERHOOD (IRB)

The IRB was founded in Dublin on St Patrick's Day 1858, following contacts between James Stephens, who had returned to Ireland in 1856, and John O'Mahony, leader of the Irish republicans in New York. Both were 1848 veterans who had shared exile in France, mixing with the various European radicals and revolutionaries who thronged Paris between 1848 and 1851. Stephens was the chief organiser and undisputed leader of the

5.

6.

new movement, which was initially nameless — the title IRB was adopted later. He was ably assisted by another 1848 man, Thomas Clarke Luby, who attended the inaugural meeting in Dublin and helped formulate the membership oath. The oath was simple: 'I, A B, in the presence of the Almighty God, do solemnly swear allegiance to the Irish Republic, now virtually established, and that I will do my very utmost at every risk, while life lasts, to defend its independence and integrity; and, finally, that I will yield implicit obedience in all things, not contrary to the laws of God, to the commands of my superior officers. So help me God. Amen.'

The aim was equally simple, to establish an independent Irish republic by physical force. History had shown, it was felt, that Britain would 'never concede self-government to the force of argument but only to the argument of force' and that therefore parliamentary politics were futile and demoralising. Meanwhile constitutional nationalists strove to re-launch the movement for self rule, among a dispirited and traumatised people. The overlapping and occasional alliance between constitutional nationalists campaigning for Home Rule within the British empire and republicans seeking an independent state, was to continue up to the Great War. Both groups became deeply involved in the other major issue of the time, land reform. Later, all three strands — constitutional, agrarian and revolutionary

Photo 7. Thomas Clarke Luby (1822–1901). Born in Dublin, he was a founder member of the IRB in 1858 and a major contributor to the Irish People *in the 1860s. Jailed in 1865 and released in 1871, after which he settled in America.*

Photo 8. Terence Bellew McManus, a Young Ireland leader, was transported to Van Diemen's Land after 1848, but escaped to America in 1853. Following his death in 1861, his body was returned to Ireland and his funeral was the occasion of huge public demonstrations, providing a major boost for the IRB.

7.

8.

Photo 9. John O'Leary (1830–1907). A Young Irelander imprisoned briefly in 1848, he became one of the most influential writers and thinkers in the Fenian movement. In 1863 he became editor of the Irish People *and was jailed in 1865. After his release in the 1870s he settled in Paris, returning to Dublin in 1885.*

Photo 10. Jeremiah O'Donovan Rossa (1831–1915). Born in Rosscarbery, Co Cork, he joined the IRB in 1858 and became business editor of the Irish People *in 1863. He was arrested in 1865 and ill-treated while in jail. Amnestied in 1871, he went to America, from where he launched a 'dynamite campaign' at English cities in the 1880s.*

— coalesced for a time under the leadership of Charles Stewart Parnell, during the so-called 'New Departure' of the 1880s.

Stephens, Luby and their associates immediately made contact with other like-minded groups and individuals. There was in existence already a nucleus of committed republicans, especially among the artisans of Dublin and Kilkenny, and in organisations such as the Phoenix Society in west Cork. However, the new movement was to find its greatest support among 'small farmers and labourers, soldiers, schoolmasters, clerks, shop assistants and urban workers generally. . . . they wrote off the landed aristocracy as a whole, were suspicious of the well-to-do middle class and pinned their faith to the common man'. The IRB was organised in cells, similar to contemporary secret societies in Europe. It spread slowly at first, but 1861 proved a turning point. In that year Terence Bellew McManus, an 1848 veteran, died in California, and his remains were returned to Ireland. The funeral, organised by the IRB, was an occasion of huge public demonstrations of sympathy, which boosted recruitment dramatically. In 1863 the IRB launched its own newspaper, the *Irish People*, which proved extremely influential in gaining new members and spreading republican principles. Apart from Luby, its chief contributors were John O'Leary, Charles Kickham and Jeremiah O'Donovan Rossa, all of whom were to become important figures in the movement later.

PLOTTING REBELLION 1860–67

Following a period of recruitment, arming and drilling, the long-awaited rising was planned for 1865. By this stage the IRB was estimated to be 100,000 strong, but was poorly equipped. Arms were procured in various ways. One of the most audacious was the open purchase of firearms in Britain by Ricard O'Sullivan Burke, a colourful veteran of the American Civil War, posing as an agent of the Chilean government. Guns were also acquired from sympathisers in the British Army itself, where by the mid 1860s there were an estimated 15,000 Fenians, recruited by agents such as Patrick 'Pagan' O'Leary, John Devoy, William Roantree and John Boyle O'Reilly. O'Leary was a veteran of the American/Mexican war of 1847; Roantree had served in the US Navy and fought in Nicaragua; Devoy had gained his military experience in the French Foreign Legion; and O'Reilly had enlisted in the British Army for the express purpose of recruiting Fenians.

As the plans for insurrection intensified, a considerable number of Irish veterans of the American Civil War made their way to Ireland and Britain in preparation for action. Funding from America increased. The sheer success of people such as Devoy in gaining recruits had, however, made

Photo 11. Ricard O'Sullivan Burke (1838–1922). A native of Co Cork and American Civil War veteran, he played an important part in Fenian activities in Britain, including the Manchester rescue of September 1867. Imprisoned in Clerkenwell, Woking and Broadmoor, he was released in 1872.

Photo 12. John Boyle O'Reilly (1844–90). Born at Dowth, Co Meath, he joined the British Army in order to recruit Fenians. Arrested in 1866 and sentenced to life imprisonment, but escaped from Dartmoor. Re-captured and transported to Australia, he escaped again in 1869 on an American whaler. A writer, poet and journalist, he became editor of the influential Boston Pilot *newspaper.*

*Photo 13
Composite
illustration entitled
'The Irish Fenian
executive', with
below, a hundred
dollar Fenian bond.*

THE IRISH FENIAN EXECUTIVE.

*Photo 14. (Facing
page) Anti-Fenian
cartoon, 1867. The
involvement of large
numbers of Irish-
Americans in the
events of 1865–67
caused considerable
anger and unease in
Britain, particularly
since American
citizens had to be
treated more
sensitively than Irish
'felons'.*

secrecy virtually impossible. The movement, at home and abroad, was infiltrated by informers, some close to the leadership. As Stephens and his lieutenants finalised their plans, the authorities swooped in September 1865 and arrested many of the leaders. The principal recruiters in the British Army, such as John Boyle O'Reilly, were rounded up soon afterwards and the 'contaminated' regiments posted abroad. Stephens was arrested but escaped from Richmond prison in a daring rescue planned by two men who were to figure prominently in the subsequent history of Fenianism, John Devoy and Thomas J Kelly. His authority within the movement was, however, irretrievably damaged.

Photo 15. John Devoy in prison garb, 1866. The arrest of Devoy and other leaders in 1865 and 1866 made an organised rising impossible.

16.

14.

15.

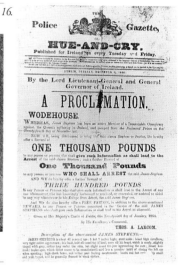

The difficulties faced by the IRB at this point were exacerbated by a split in the American organisation. One faction, led by John O'Mahony, wished to channel all available funds directly into an Irish insurrection. Another wing, impatient with postponements and failures in Ireland, began to plan for an Irish-American invasion of Canada.

The widespread arrests and deportations of figures such as John Boyle O'Reilly, John Devoy and Joseph Deneiffe crippled the IRB. A small hard-core determined to go ahead with a rising, however, but when it did take place in the spring of 1867 it was a total failure. Uncoordinated uprisings

Photo 16. Proclamation offering one thousand pounds for the capture of James Stephens, January 1866. Stephens' escape from Richmond Prison was facilitated by Fenians in the prison service.

Photo 17. (Above left) A skirmish between troops and Fenians, Tipperary, March 1867.

Photo 18. (Above right) The battle of Tallaght, 5 March 1867. The defeat and dispersal of the Fenians near Tallaght village was followed by the collapse of the rising in the Dublin area.

Photo 19 Courtroom scene, Kilmallock, Co Limerick, following the collapse of the Fenian rising in 1867. Kilmallock was the scene of considerable fighting between Fenians and constabulary.

in the Iveragh peninsula of Co Kerry in February and in south Dublin in March were easily suppressed, as were minor attempts in Cork, Waterford and Tipperary around the same time. In the Dublin fighting, the constabulary barracks of Stepaside and Glencullen were captured, but the rout of the main Fenian body at Tallaght was followed by the dispersal and arrest of most of the participants. In Cork, attacks on Midleton and Castlemartyr failed, as did the attempt to capture Kilmallock barracks in Co Limerick. The last episode in the confused saga of heroism and inefficiency was still to come. Believing that fighting was still going on in

Ireland, John O'Mahony's group in New York fitted out a small vessel, the *Jackmel*, which sailed from that city on 12 April 1867 with several thousand Springfield rifles and forty military veterans aboard. At sea she hoisted the Irish flag and changed her name to *Erin's Hope*. Arriving in Sligo Bay on 20 May, the ship was boarded by the indomitable Ricard O'Sullivan Burke, described by John Devoy as 'by long odds the most remarkable man the Fenian movement produced'. Burke carried with him the heartbreaking news that the rising was over. The captain sailed his ship half way round the country before landing his passengers near Dungarvan, Co Waterford, where most of them were promptly arrested. The ship, with cargo intact, sailed back to America. She had come, in the words of John Devoy, 'two years too late'.

Photo 20. The Erin's Hope, 1867. The arms ship took over five weeks to reach Ireland, but the journey was in vain. The rising was over before she left New York.

James Stephens, his credibility damaged beyond repair, had by now been replaced by a more militant group, back-boned by American Civil War veterans and determined to fight on regardless of the odds. Some of the most dramatic exploits of this group were carried out, not in Ireland, but in England.

THE FENIANS IN ENGLAND

Fenianism spread to England at an early stage, gaining a strong following not only among emigrant Irish labourers and artisans, but also among second-generation Irish. It even gained the sympathy of some of the English working-class movements and was seen by some commentators as the natural ally of the radical movements that led to the formation of the Labour Party. Fenian leaders in England were on friendly terms with Karl Marx and Friedrich Engels, who were keenly interested in Irish affairs. There were Fenian cells in the major cities, and the movement was particularly strong in Lancashire.

Following the 1865 debacle and the lack of action in 1866, a body of English-based activists and Irish-American officers, led by Thomas Kelly, Ricard O'Sullivan Burke and John McCafferty, drew up a daring plan to spearhead a rising from England. The audacious scheme involved a surprise attack on the military arsenal in Chester, to be followed by the

THE FENIAN-PEST.

Photo 21. Anti-Fenian cartoon, 1866.

Photo 22. The rescue of Colonel Thomas Kelly and Captain Timothy Deasy, Manchester, September 1867 (from Illustrated London News, *1867). The death of a police sergeant during the rescue provoked considerable anti-Irish feeling in Britain.*

commandeering of the mailboat or other shipping in Holyhead and the transportation of the captured arms to Ireland. The plan was betrayed to the authorities and had to be aborted, but the strength of the organisation may be measured from the fact that over one thousand English Fenians from Liverpool, Leeds, Bradford, Halifax and other towns, turned out on the appointed day. Among them was a young one-armed man carrying a bag of bullets. His name was Michael Davitt, who was to claim his place in Irish history as the founder of the Land League.

The Chester fiasco was followed by the arrest of Captain McCafferty. In September Colonel Kelly, now head of the IRB following the demotion of Stephens, was arrested in Manchester with another Irish-American officer, Captain Deasy. A fortnight later both men were rescued from a prison van in broad daylight. A policeman was shot dead during the rescue. Three of those arrested in the subsequent police round-up, William Allen, Michael Larkin and Michael O'Brien, were sentenced to death and hanged on 23 November. They had been part of the rescue party, but none had fired the fatal shot. They were hanged essentially to placate public opinion, and their executions caused outrage even among those most vehemently opposed to Fenianism. The song 'God Save Ireland', composed in their memory, was to become one of the best known of all republican anthems.

cont. p 33

Pl 1. Handkerchief
commemorating
Daniel O'Connell's
victory in the Clare
election, 1828.
O'Connell's success
in Clare brought the
issue of Catholic
emancipation to a
head and was a
major factor in
influencing the
British government
to grant
emancipation in
1829.

Pl 2. Gold cup
presented to William
Smith O'Brien.
O'Brien was
transported to
Tasmania following
the unsuccessful
1848 rising. This
magnificent gold cup
was presented to him
by the Irish residents
of Melbourne and
Geelong on his
release in 1854,
prior to his return to
Ireland.

Pl 3. Flag captured from the Fenians at Tallaght, March 1867. The design, influenced by the American 'stars and stripes', shows thirty-two stars, representing Ireland's thirty-two counties.

Pl 4. Fenian flags. Reconstructions from descriptions given by contemporaries during the trials of 1865 and 1866.

Pl 5. Fenian bond for twenty dollars, signed by John O'Mahony, 1866. The Irish community in America were among the most dedicated supporters of Irish independence. The IRB, the Land League, the Gaelic League, the Irish Parliamentary Party and Sinn Féin all received financial support from America.

Pl 6. Fenian bond for five dollars, 1866. Both wings of the Fenian Brotherhood issued bonds for fund-raising purposes.

Pl 7. Fenian bond certificate, undated, printed in New York.

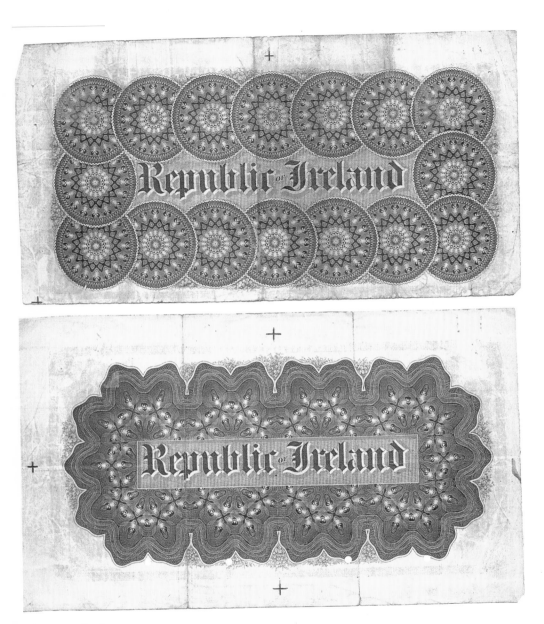

*Pl 8. Fenian bond
or note, undated.*

Under I Edward VII, Cap. 6.

This is to Certify

that _Henry Pulty Timmerman_

having served as a _Bandsman_ in _The Forty Seventh Battalion_

in _Ontario_ in _1870_ on the occasion of _The Fenian Raid_

is hereby authorized to enter upon and occupy _The North Half_

of _Lot Number Seven_ in the _Fifth_ concession

of the Township of _Lucas_ containing _160½_ acres,

under and subject to the provisions of said Act.

Given under my hand at Toronto

this _Fifteenth_ day of _April_ A.D. 190_7_

Commissioner of Crown Lands.

Countersigned _A. Browne_

Pl 9. Location certificate and land grant to a Canadian militia veteran who served against the Fenians in 1870. The attacks against Canada between 1866 and 1871 kept the authorities in a state of apprehension, strained Anglo-American relations, and led to 'Fenian fever' in the media.

Pl 10. Flag of the Catalpa, the ship that was used to rescue Fenian prisoners from Freemantle in 1876. The New Bedford whaler hoisted the American flag as soon as the escaped prisoners were aboard.

Pl 11. The escape of the Freemantle prisoners, April 1876. The daring rescue, planned by Clan na Gael in America, was aided by IRB members, Australian sympathisers, and even funding from New Zealand.

Pl 12. Anti-Fenian cartoon, New York, 1881. The tendency of American Fenians to disagree and split over tactics and strategy remained a problem throughout the period.

Pl 13. Anti-O'Donovan Rossa cartoon, New York, 1882. O'Donovan Rossa's brainchild of a 'dynamite campaign' aimed at government and public buildings in Britain was opposed by many Fenians, who regarded it as futile.

14(a).

14(b).

15.

Pl 14. *Sections of a Land League flag from Kilmaley, Co Clare, depicting Parnell and Davitt. Both men were indispensable to the success of the Land League, but it was Davitt's standing and influence that ensured the all-important support of rank-and-file Fenians, in Ireland and America.*

Pl 15. *Home Rule cartoon, 1880s. Parnell gained the support of great numbers of Fenians at home and abroad as a result of his aggressive political stance and his ability to combine parliamentary and extra-parliamentary agitation.*

Pl 16. Political cartoon (Weekly Freeman, 25 February 1882). The totally unequal nature of the landlord/tenant relationship was a major cause of the land war. Evictions were resisted by what became known as boycotting — the total social and economic ostracisation of landlords, their agents and anyone attempting to replace evicted tenants.

Pl 17. Political cartoon (Weekly Freeman, 6 October 1883). Constitutional nationalists regularly made the point that the refusal of the British to accept their moderate demands made violence and insurrection inevitable, and vindicated those who were willing to assert rights by force.

FREEDOM OF CONTRACT—IN IRELAND.

DRIVING HIM UNDER THE SURFACE.

18.

SUPPLEMENT GIVEN AWAY WITH THE WEEKLY FREEMAN OF MARCH 17th 1883 PRICE THREE HALF-PENCE

A SEVERE ATTACK.

CHILDREN OF ERIN—"Oh, Mother! Has that animal gone mad?"
ERIN—"Yes, my dear children. He is in one of his periodical Anti-Irish frenzies; but don't be frightened—he will cool down presently. We will survive this attack as we have many a one before."

19.

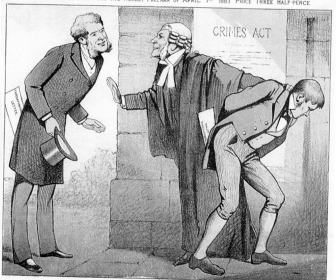

SUPPLEMENT GIVEN AWAY WITH THE WEEKLY FREEMAN OF APRIL 7th 1883 PRICE THREE HALF-PENCE

"EQUAL BEFORE THE LAW." (on Paper.)

LANDLORD and J.P. to CROWN LAWYER—"My dear Sir, there are some officious people annoying me, and are menacing me with legal consequences because I wrote a threatening letter to an internal tenant of mine."
CROWN LAWYER—"Be reassured, my dear Landlord. You shall suffer no inconvenience from the law;—not like this scoundrel of a tenant, who wrote an intemperate note to his landlord. I will get him two years hard labour to teach him civility."

Pls 18–21.
Nationalist political
cartoons, 1883.
Newspaper cartoons
of the period were
fiercely partisan on
both the nationalist
and unionist sides.
The great issues of
the day — land
reform, Home Rule
and the rival claims
of nationalists and
unionists, were all
the subject of
scathing pictorial
treatment.

20.

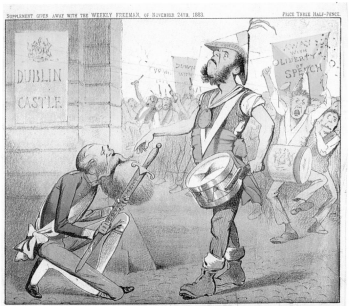

SUPPLEMENT GIVEN AWAY WITH THE WEEKLY FREEMAN OF SEPTEMBER 22ND, 1883. PRICE THREE HALF-PENCE.

COERCION

NATIONAL LEAGUE IN AMERICA

THE LAND FOR THE PEOPLE

GLADSTONE'S ACT A FAILURE

HERE LIES
THE REMAINS
OF THE
IRISH LAND AGITATION
WHICH SUCCUMBED
TO THE FIRMNESS
OF A SPENSER
AND THE WISDOM
OF A GLADSTONE
R.I.P.

LAND BILL

A MOCK BURIAL.

FIRST GRAVE-DIGGER TO LOOKER-ON.—"Hallo ! What brings you about again; don't you know that the Land Question is satisfactorily settled for ever, and that all the agitation connected with it is dead and buried under this stone."
HIMSELF.—"I know no such thing; and I can only tell you that you are living in a fool's Paradise if you think that it will ever die until every Farmer in Ireland owns the farm he tills."
[This will spoil a good many Snoozlets of a certain old Gentleman during the Recess.]

21.

SUPPLEMENT GIVEN AWAY WITH THE WEEKLY FREEMAN, OF NOVEMBER 24TH, 1883. PRICE THREE HALF-PENCE.

DUBLIN CASTLE

DOWN WITH

DOWN WITH

AWAY WITH LIBERTY OF SPEECH

SURRENDER AND NO SURRENDER.

ORANGE LEADER (aside to follower).—"Play up as loud as you can and fire a volley or two, to frighten him." To HIGH OFFICIAL—" Look here ! Hand over that sword to us and we will never show you nor others, how to use it—with a vengeance."
HIGH OFFICIAL—"My dear Sir, I will obey you in anything you command ; but would it not appear better if I seemed to be in possession of this weapon whilst you really used it." [Suggestion adopted]

Pl 22. Nationalist cartoon, 1887. The golden jubilee of Queen Victoria's reign was an occasion of great public celebration in Britain, while in Ireland it was a time of land agitation, coercion acts and evictions. After eighty-seven years of Union, Ireland was said to be 'distracted, disloyal and impoverished'.

Pl 23. Membership certificate, Wolfe Tone Memorial Association. The IRB used the centenary of the 1798 rising as an opportunity to reawaken public interest in the principles of republicanism, to gain new recruits and to revitalise the organisation. John O'Leary was president.

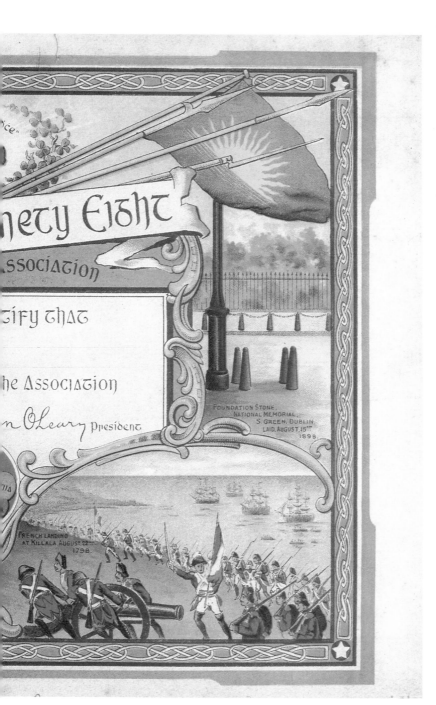

FRENCH LANDING AT KILLALA AUGUST 22 1798.

FOUNDATION STONE, NATIONAL MEMORIAL, S. GREEN, DUBLIN. LAID, AUGUST, 15TH 1898.

Pl 24. (Following page) Major John MacBride, 1865–1916 (from a charcoal sketch by Seán O'Sullivan). Born in Westport, Co Mayo, he joined the IRB in the 1880s and was involved in the formation of the GAA. Fought in the Boer War with the Irish Brigade. Married Maud Gonne, republican activist and organiser, 1903. Fought in 1916, was court-martialled, and executed on 5 May 1916.

Pl 25. (Page 31) Tom Clarke, 1857–1916 (from a charcoal sketch by Seán O'Sullivan). Born on the Isle of Wight, he joined Clan na Gael in America, was arrested in England during the dynamite campaign in 1883, and spent fifteen years in jail. He returned to Ireland in 1907 to re-organise the IRB and plan for insurrection. The first and oldest signatory of the Proclamation of Independence, he was executed on 3 May 1916.

4.

cont. from p 16

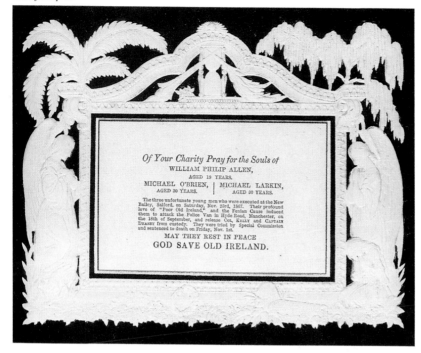

Photo 23.
Manchester Martyrs
memorial card,
1867. The public
executions of Allen,
Larkin and O'Brien
caused an
international outcry,
and protest meetings
were held as far
away as South
Africa and New
Zealand.

Of Your Charity Pray for the Souls of
WILLIAM PHILIP ALLEN,
AGED 19 YEARS.
MICHAEL O'BRIEN, | MICHAEL LARKIN,
AGED 30 YEARS. | AGED 20 YEARS.

The three unfortunate young men who were executed at the New Bailey, Salford, on Saturday, Nov. 23rd, 1867. Their profound love of "Poor Old Ireland," and the Fenian Cause induced them to attack the Police Van in Hyde Road, Manchester, on the 18th of September, and release COX, KELLY and CAPTAIN DEASEY from custody. They were tried by Special Commission and sentenced to death on Friday, Nov. 1st.

MAY THEY REST IN PEACE
GOD SAVE OLD IRELAND.

The leader of the Manchester rescue, Ricard O'Sullivan Burke, was himself arrested and lodged in Clerkenwell Prison, London, from which an attempt was made to rescue him in December 1867. The gunpowder explosion that blew a huge hole in the prison wall failed to free Burke but killed several people in adjoining tenements. It sparked off a wave of public and media hysteria and brought Irish issues onto the streets of Britain. In the longer term the conviction and resilience that sustained Fenianism was to have a major influence on contemporary politicians and commentators, and especially on William Gladstone, the Liberal prime minister, who was to become a life-long advocate of Home Rule for Ireland.

THE FENIAN BROTHERHOOD AND THE INVASION OF CANADA

Numerous societies, social and political, sprang up among the Irish in America, especially after the exodus that followed the famine and the failure of the 1848 rebellion. In the early 1850s the principal Young Ireland

*Pl 26. (Facing page)
John Daly (from a
charcoal sketch by
Seán O'Sullivan). A
fellow-prisoner and
friend of Tom Clark,
he spent twelve years
in jail for his part in
the dynamite
campaign of the
1880s. Mayor of
Limerick, 1901–3.*

refugees, such as John O'Mahony and Michael Doheny, were joined by John Mitchel and Thomas Francis Meagher, both of whom escaped from the convict settlement on Van Diemen's Land (Tasmania), where they had been imprisoned. Preparations for rebellion in Ireland got under way. As early as 1848 a military club, the Irish Republican Union, filled with veterans of the recent Mexican War, had threatened to invade Canada, but faded away following the collapse of the rising in Ireland. The outbreak of the Crimean War in 1854, however, raised expectations again and a new organisation, the Emmet Monument Society, was formed in 1855. A representative was sent to Ireland to assess the possibility of an armed rising while Britain was at war with Russia. The Russian consul in New York was approached in the hope of securing transport to Ireland for two thousand men, and guns for a further five thousand. With the end of the Crimean War, the society went into abeyance, but from it emerged the people who were to launch the Fenian Brotherhood a few years later. The possibility of conflict between Britain and France in 1859/60, and between Britain and the US during and after the Civil War, fuelled hopes of a successful insurrection.

The launching of the IRB in 1858 was followed a few months later by the formal setting up of the Fenian Brotherhood in the United States. Its principal leaders, such as John O'Mahony and Michael Doheny, were committed revolutionaries who were determined that the fiasco of 1848 would not be repeated. The name, from the legendary warriors of Irish mythology, the *Fianna*, came eventually to be applied in a general way to republicans on both sides of the Atlantic.

The existence of two separate organisations was to cause considerable friction and misunderstanding. The Irish tended to regard their American colleagues as auxiliaries, whose function was to provide finance and arms. The Americans, however, were unwilling to accept a subordinate role. This conflict, never properly resolved, was to surface at intervals right into the 1920s.

In the meantime the Brotherhood rapidly expanded. The outbreak of the American Civil War temporarily thinned its ranks as members became involved, largely on the Union side, in the conflict. On the other hand the

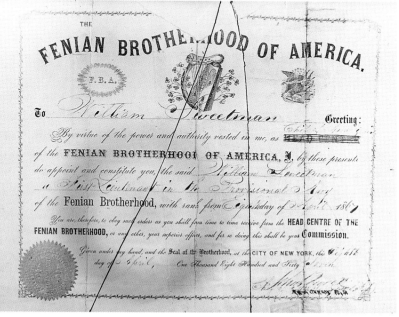

Photo 24. General
Thomas Francis
Meagher and the
Irish Brigade at the
Battle of Fair Oaks,
1862. The
American Civil War
provided valuable
military training for
the Fenians.

Photo 25.
Commission
appointing William
Sweetman as a First
Lieutenant in the
Provisional Navy of
the Fenian
Brotherhood, 1867.

war provided a whole generation of Irish-American military veterans who joined the organisation in great numbers at the conclusion of hostilities. The dangers of military action in Ireland, Canada or elsewhere, held little fear for soldiers who had survived one of the bloodiest wars of all times.

The failure of the IRB to launch the promised rising of 1865, together with policy disagreements between the leaders, led to a split in the Brotherhood. O'Mahony's group wished to channel all available resources to Ireland. His opponents, the so-called 'senate' wing, decided to invade Canada, encouraged by the ready availability of armed men, the geographical proximity of the enemy and the belief that the strained relations between Washington and London would ensure at very least the benevolent neutrality of the US.

The attack on Canada was planned as a three-pronged assault, from

Photo 26. The battle of Limestone Ridge, Ontario, June 1866. The raids on Canada were militarily insignificant, but gained considerable international attention for the Fenian cause.

Vermont in the east, Buffalo in the centre and Chicago in the west. Overall command of the operation was given to Brigadier General Thomas Sweeney, a veteran of both the Mexican/American conflict of 1847 and the Civil War, who had distinguished himself at the Battle of Shiloh in 1862. Canadian Fenians were to seize bridges and cut communications. Like so many other Fenian projects, a plan that had considerable prospects in theory collapsed in the execution. Lack of co-ordination, ineptitude and the action of the American government in sealing the frontier doomed the plan to failure. The western attack never got off the ground. In the centre Colonel John O'Neill led a Fenian force across the frontier north of Buffalo and occupied the village of Fort Erie. Cut off from reinforcements and low on ammunition, O'Neill was soon forced to retreat, but not before his men had routed a force of Canadian militia at the battle of Limestone Ridge, on 2 June 1866.

Photo 27. (Facing page) Fenian prisoners at exercise break in Mountjoy prison, Dublin. The collapse of the 1867 rising was followed by wholesale arrests and deportations.

Photo 28. (Facing page) Tipperary election address, 1869. The election of O'Donovan Rossa, then a high-profile Fenian prisoner in Chatham jail, was a major propaganda boost for the amnesty movement.

A few days later a force of one thousand badly armed Fenians under General Speer crossed the frontier from Vermont, but were immediately driven back. As in the case of O'Neill's force, they were disarmed by the American authorities. A second attempt by O'Neill in 1870 from New York and Vermont was even less successful, again due to the usual combination of informers and poor organisation. The irrepressible O'Neill launched a last attack across the frontier in 1871, briefly seizing the small town of Pembina, Manitoba. This was the last defiant gesture of 'old style' Fenianism. By this stage the rival wings of American Fenianism were in the process of being reunited under a new association, Clan na Gael (The Irish Race), which was to become the most effective and long-lasting of Irish-American republican organisations. Led by such figures as John Devoy and Dr William Carroll, it was to provide invaluable financial and moral support to every Irish nationalist society for half a century.

AMNESTY

Following the debacles of 1865–67, the various strands of Fenianism began the slow process of reorganisation. The Catholic hierarchy, with few exceptions, was fiercely hostile. The bishop of Kerry, who regarded Fenianism as a godless conspiracy, threatened 'God's heaviest curse, his withering, blasting, blighting curse'. Fenians were refused the sacraments, and in 1870 Pope Pius IX condemned the organisation by name. Fenians such as Charles Kickham demanded in turn that the church should keep out of politics. Kickham's quotation from Fr Luke Wadding, a seventeenth-century scholar, 'Time was when we had wooden chalices and golden priests but now we have golden chalices and wooden priests', raised temperatures further. The plight of Fenian prisoners, in jails on three continents, provided a focus and rallying point. The US government was lobbied to intercede for

O'DONOVAN ROSSA
FOR TIPPERARY.
ADDRESS OF THE FRIENDS OF AMNESTY,
TO THE ELECTORS OF TIPPERARY.

Men of Tipperary. Gallantly and nobly have you espoused the cause of your suffering brethren. Well and truly do you interpret the feelings that swell to bursting the full heart of Ireland mourning for her cruelly tortured children. Most heartily do we approve of your choice.

Unto death, and in sufferings far worse than the most dreadful death have those noble hearted men proved their unselfish love of Motherland. What tongue can tell, what words describe the mental tortures that have unseated reason from her throne? What the physical sufferings from which so many victims have found refuge in the grave? "Greater love than this no man "hath, that a man lay down his life for his friend." Even more than life have those men laid down for their country. For we are assured by one who suffered that he would far rather meet death than endure for one three months what he suffered in prison! What love then does not Ireland owe them in return? Nor has She been unmindful of them—but, humbling herself in the dust— the Petition of the Nation for their release containing 250,000 names was laid at the feet of the Queen. Her humble petition was spurned with contempt. For months the Nation mourned in silence. Again she aroused herself to another effort on behalf of her suffering sons; and at the Amnesty Meetings the full heart of the country sent up to Heaven the cry of Ireland mourning for her children because they are not. And once again the prayer of Ireland meets only the heart- less denial of the English Minister and the threats and scoffs of the English Press. And now, ere she folds her hands in solemn and dignified silence, leaving the cause of outraged humanity to God and the civilized world. Ireland, by the voice of noble, gallant Tipperary, places on record her protest against the treatment of the Political Prisoners, and proclaims to the world that the English Ministers' cruel refusal to release them from their tortures, has intensified her love for them; and that their names shall henceforth be enshrined in the hearts of their countrymen, and become the watchword and the rallying cry to which the Nation shall be roused to action.

Electors of Tipperary, nobly have you responded to the wishes of the Nation. By inscribing on banner and shield "Rossa for Tipperary," you proclaim to the world how dear to the heart of Ireland he and his companions in suffering have become. You stand before the world as their and Ireland's champion. To you, they and Ireland commit a sacred cause—a sublime duty. It is for you, men, of Tipperary, to rise equal to the distinguished part you are now about to play in the History of your Country. The Tipperary election of 1869 shall be an epoch in Irish History, and shall be memorable to all future generations of Irishmen.

In the name of God and of our suffering countrymen—in the name of humanity and of Ireland, we call upon you Men, of Tipperary, to prove yourselves equal to the proud position the voice of Ireland assigns to you, by electing O'Donovan Rossa as the MOST FITTING person to represent you.

GOD SAVE IRELAND?

NOVEMBER 10th, 1869.

p. 37/155

Fenian prisoners in Canada. In Ireland an Amnesty Association, which included many constitutional nationalists and whose president was Isaac Butt, founder of the Home Rule movement, agitated for the release of prisoners and highlighted the ill-treatment suffered by many. Conditions in British prisons at the time have been described as 'harsh to the point of being sadistic'. In two years, seven Fenians died in jail, four committed suicide and four went totally insane. One prisoner, Jeremiah O'Donovan Rossa, spent '123 days on a bread and water punishment diet, 231 days on a penal class diet in a darkened cell, 28 days in a completely dark cell and 34 days with his hands manacled behind his back, after this he was occasionally punished for singing'. At his trial, he had been accused of the ultimate evil, 'inciting the lower orders to believe that they might expect a redistribution of property'. While in prison he was elected member of parliament for Tipperary, further highlighting the plight of those jailed. In Britain, an Amnesty Committee held parades and public meetings, demanding the release of those incarcerated. Political figures, workingmen's associations and international radicals joined together in what was an unusual display of solidarity. Among the most vocal was Karl Marx. The government relented and began to release prisoners. Leaders such as John Devoy, O'Donovan Rossa and Thomas Clarke Luby were released in 1871, but only on condition that they should not return to Ireland. Most of them headed immediately for America. Fenians were also released in Australia, some of whom followed their comrades to America.

Photo 29. The 'Cuba Five', amnestied in 1871. John Devoy, Charles Underwood O'Connell, Henry Mulleda, Jeremiah O'Donovan Rossa and John McClure. Named after the steamship that took them to America, they received a huge public welcome in New York.

The guard-boat   The whaleboat with escaping prisoners   The Georgette

THE *CATALPA* RESCUE

One group of prisoners was refused release, despite the amnesty campaign. These were the so-called 'soldier Fenians' in Freemantle prison, western Australia, who had been serving members of the British Army. One of these, John Boyle O'Reilly, had escaped on board a whaling ship in 1869 (he had earlier escaped from Dartmoor in England but had been recaptured). One of the Freemantle prisoners managed to contact one of the released Fenians in New York in 1871, with a plea for rescue. The matter was placed in the hands of John Devoy and plans were made to free the prisoners from their 'servitude in one of the darkest corners of the earth'. It was a slow and difficult task. Funds were raised, a whaling ship was purchased, and advice received from Fenians who had already escaped from Australia. Finally, in

Photo 30. John Devoy, organiser of the Catalpa *rescue.*

Photo 31. John J Breslin, leader of the Catalpa *rescue mission. Described by John Devoy as 'a man of fine presence, good manners, high intelligence and very unusual decision of character'.*

Photo 32. Thomas J Desmond, second in command to John J Breslin on the Catalpa *rescue mission. Proposed by the California Clan na Gael, he proved to be a brave and valuable assistant.*

Photo 33. James Reynolds, 'Catalpa Jim', a member of the rescue committee. The rescue plans, coordinated by John Devoy, entailed the raising of considerable sums of money.

Photo 34. Illustration entitled 'The Race for the Catalpa'. The escaped prisoners and their rescuers reached the Catalpa *a few hundred yards ahead of the pursuing police vessel.*

*Photo 35. The six
Fenian prisoners
rescued from
Freemantle, 1876,
pictured following
their arrival in
America.*

*Photo 36. The
Catalpa rescue.
Illustration from a
pamphlet by John
Denvir, 1882.*

April 1875, the whaler *Catalpa,* under a reliable sea captain, George Anthony, sailed out of New Bedford, Massachusetts, on an epic voyage which took her, via the Azores, to the coast of western Australia, arriving on 28 March 1876. The actual escape was planned and carried out by a group already in place under John Breslin (who had master-minded the release of James Stephens over a decade earlier), aided by Australian Fenians. The escape took place on 17 April and was followed by a dramatic dash in an open whaleboat. After twenty-eight hours at sea, the six prisoners scrambled onto the *Catalpa,* just as they were about to be intercepted by a police cutter. A police steamer arrived to prevent the withdrawal of the *Catalpa,* threatening to blow her masts off. Anthony's reply 'That's the American flag . . . if you fire on this ship, you fire on the United States' deterred the police. The *Catalpa* sailed back to America, where the captain, crew and released prisoners received a tumultuous welcome on their arrival in New York on 19 August 1876. The rescue was a huge morale booster for Fenians world-wide. Back in Australia the *Freemantle Herald* noted that the escape gave 'infinite satisfaction to the masses'.

As the decade progressed, the leadership continued to watch, wait and monitor the international situation. In the late 1870s when it appeared that Britain and Russia might go to war, Clan na Gael sought Russian support for an Irish rising, but in vain. Around the same period the Spanish government was approached with a Fenian offer to capture Gibraltar for Spain. The Spaniards politely refused. John Holland, the Irish inventor and 'father' of the modern submarine, was generously funded by Devoy and his colleagues in the expectation that his invention might prove useful against British shipping. One of Holland's early prototypes was christened *The Fenian Ram.* There was even a suggestion that guns should be smuggled to the Zulus in South Africa, in their fight against British colonial expansion. Some of the schemes were audacious, some were naïve, but they all had a single objective — to attack and embarrass British interests wherever possible. The 1880s also witnessed a 'dynamite campaign' in Britain by two different Fenian factions, one led by O'Donovan Rossa, the other by Clan na Gael, at a time when Devoy had temporarily lost control of that organisation. Both campaigns petered out without achieving anything. By this stage, however, political and social developments had turned Fenianism in new directions.

THE LAND LEAGUE

The Land League was founded by Michael Davitt in 1879, at a time when crop failures and agricultural recession were causing massive hardship, especially among the smaller farmers and farm labourers. It was launched

Photo 37. Michael Davitt (1846–1906). Born at Straide, Co Mayo, he moved to Lancashire as a boy, losing an arm in a factory accident when eleven years old. IRB organiser and founder of the Land League, he worked unremittingly to abolish landlordism. Described as 'a rare combination of revolutionary, reformer, idealist, realist, dogmatist, pragmatist'.

Photo 38. Battering ram used during eviction, 1880s. The inability of tenants to pay rent during the agricultural recession led to an upsurge in evictions, sometimes carried out with great harshness.

Photo 39. Land League poster, 1881–82. The banning of the League in 1881, together with the imprisonment of Parnell and Davitt, led to an intensification of agrarian violence.

Photo 40. Land League manifesto, 1881. The passing of a coercion act, the suppression of the Land League and the arrest of Parnell was countered by a 'no rent' manifesto. Patrick Egan moved to Paris, from where he directed the financial affairs of the League.

Photo 41. Eviction scene, November 1880. The misery and anger caused by forced evictions hardened the opposition to landlordism.

Photo 42. Eviction scene, undated.

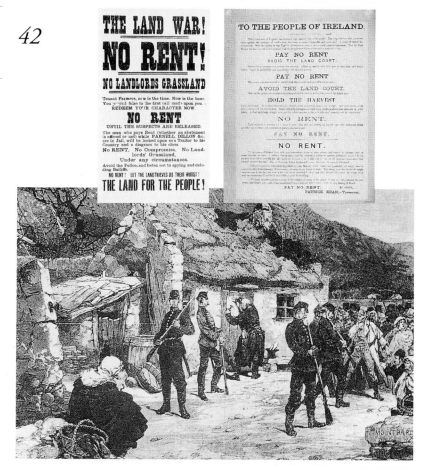

primarily as a tenants' defence association to oppose the excesses and unfair demands of landlords. Davitt had spent seven years in Dartmoor for his activities as a Fenian armaments officer in England. Following his release he went to America where he formulated with John Devoy a new policy of self-government and land reform. This took shape in 1879 as the 'New Departure', an alliance of republicans, agrarian reformers and constitutional nationalists, which encountered strong opposition from 'old guard' Fenians such as John O'Leary and Charles Kickham. The third side of the triangle fell into place when Devoy met and made an informal agreement with Charles Stewart Parnell, leader of the Irish Parliamentary Party. Davitt's astute move in offering the presidency of the Land League to Parnell ushered in a new era in Irish politics. The organisation 'combined in one great agrarian movement all nationalists from moderates to revolutionaries'. During the ensuing land-war the struggle for tenant rights developed into a demand for full ownership that was to end with the dismantling of the landlord system. As the struggle intensified through evictions, boycotting and withholding rent, many of the IRB rank and file became increasingly involved, and the Irish-Americans, through Clan na Gael, contributed substantial aid. For Davitt, the founder and guiding genius of the Land League, the slogan 'the land of Ireland for the people of Ireland' led logically to nationalisation, but in this he was far more radical than his followers, Fenians and non-Fenians alike. For the IRB leadership the League was a mixed blessing, since it diverted attention from what the organisation saw as the prime objective, political independence.

Photo 43. Patrick Egan (1841–1919). A prominent IRB member who supported the campaign for Home Rule. He became treasurer of the Land League and worked with Michael Davitt during the land agitation of the 1880s.

HOME RULE

With the advent of a vigorous movement for self-government initiated by Isaac Butt and developed by Charles Stewart Parnell, many Fenians came to regard Home Rule as a vehicle that would further their aims, especially when allied to the activities of the Land League. Parnell's ability to hold together the conflicting forces of land reform, constitutional politics and armed republicanism remains one of the most remarkable political feats of the century. The defeat of the 1886 Home Rule bill, however, and the disastrous split in the party following the Parnell divorce case, brought a temporary end to hopes of parliamentary success. Within the IRB the collapse of the constitutional crusade strengthened the hand of the 'old guard' who believed that Britain would never accept self-government, much less a republic, unless forced to do so.

Most accepted, however, that while Britain was at peace, rebellion was impossible. Membership fell, furthermore, following the successful conclusion of the land-war. The new landowners were in the main politically and socially conservative and in no mood to risk their recent gains for the doubtful benefits of a republic. Their war had been fought and won. There still remained, however, a nucleus of uncompromising republicans for whom land agitation and constitutional crusades were only steps on a longer road. The dramatic revival of Gaelic sport and culture was about to open up a new and fruitful field of activity.

THE IRB AND THE GAELIC REVIVAL

John O'Mahony, one of the Fenian founding fathers, was a respected Gaelic scholar. Jeremiah O'Donovan Rossa was a fluent speaker and teacher. According to John Devoy, many of the minor leaders and most rank-and-file members in Connacht and Munster were Gaelic speakers in

Photo 44. Conradh na Gaeilge (Gaelic League) membership card. Many Fenians became involved in the language revival movement.

the early years of the movement. It is hardly surprising therefore, given their political philosophy, that many Fenians were attracted to the Gaelic League. The League, founded by Douglas Hyde in 1893 to promote the revival of Gaelic language and culture, was in theory non-political, but was inevitably drawn into the political arena. It did not confine its activities to simply reviving the Gaelic language, but articulated a radical policy of cultural, political and economic independence that influenced to some degree all the groups that were later to figure in the 1916 insurrection. Many IRB activists joined its ranks. It was not, however, one-way traffic but rather a two-way exchange. Many of the most dedicated of the IRB's organisers and leaders came into the organisation from the Gaelic League, people such as Seán MacDiarmada, Thomas MacDonagh, Eamonn Ceannt and Patrick Pearse.

THE GAELIC ATHLETIC ASSOCIATION (GAA)

The Gaelic Athletic Association, founded in 1884, has been described as one of the most successful and original mass movements of its time, 'the first modern example of a great democratic movement with the attendant apparatus of committees and boards under completely Irish auspices'. Even more so than in the case of the Gaelic League, IRB members were immediately prominent in its ranks, identifying with an organisation that regarded sport as an element in the development of national identity. A new generation was emerging for whom sport, language, politics and culture complemented one another in the struggle for independence.

FROM AGITATION TO INSURRECTION 1900–16

While the cultural and literary renaissance took root, the IRB as an organisation appeared to be in the doldrums. The centenary celebrations of the 1798 Rebellion provided a morale booster, however, and the outbreak of the Boer War raised once again the possibility of exploiting Britain's difficulties abroad. An Irish Brigade was formed under a Colonel Blake, to fight on the Boer side. Second in command was Major John MacBride, an IRB member who had been associated with Michael Cusack in the foundation of the GAA. MacBride was later to be executed for his part in the 1916 Rising.

Throughout this period the IRB continued to receive financial aid from Clan na Gael. With the return of Tom Clarke to Ireland in 1907 the movement, in the words of Devoy, 'inspired by his resoluteness and singleness of purpose, began to assume new life and vigour and become an active force'. Clarke, a Clan na Gael activist who had emerged from fifteen years' imprisonment unrepentant and undeterred, formed a powerful link between the old and new generation of Fenians. The foundation of Sinn Féin by Arthur Griffith in 1905 provided a useful political outlet for the

Photo 45. Colonel John Franklin Blake, commander of the Irish Brigade, Boer War. Following the collapse of organised Boer resistance, the brigade dispersed, mainly to America.

Photo 46. Colonel Lynch's second Irish Brigade at siege of Ladysmith, Boer War.

Photo 47. A group of Chicago Irish volunteers with Major John MacBride during the Boer War.

Photo 46. Colonel Lynch's second Irish Brigade at siege of Ladysmith, Boer War.

Photo 47. A group of Chicago Irish volunteers with Major John MacBride during the Boer War.

rejuvenated organisation. The Sinn Féin policy of withdrawal from Westminster and passive resistance to British rule was hardly radical from a Fenian point of view but had considerable potential, while its policy of economic independence could not be faulted. IRB members joined the new party, and Seán MacDiarmada, one of the IRB's most dedicated activists, became a full-time Sinn Féin organiser. Meanwhile contemporary political developments were about to provide the IRB with access to the weapon it had always lacked — an open, legal military force.

As the campaign for Home Rule was renewed in 1912, the unionists, unwilling to accept electoral results or acts of parliament, proceeded to arm themselves. This in turn led to the formation of the Irish Volunteers to defend the measure, should it become law. The IRB, whose Dublin members were already drilling in anticipation of such a move, immediately stepped in to provide the leadership and back-bone of the new military body.

The outbreak of world war in 1914 provided the opportunity for which a generation of Fenians had schemed and waited — a major international conflict. Devoy and Clarke ensured the opportunity was not missed. The rising of 1916 was the culmination of sixty years of probing, planning and self-sacrifice. The single unwavering aim of total independence for which the Fenians had fought and suffered so much was now passed on to a new generation. This had been achieved despite defeat, imprisonment, ridicule and religious censure. It was their major legacy and contribution to Irish history. In the broader context, Fenianism as a political philosophy acted as a catalyst on every strand of nationalism, political, cultural and literary. To quote a twentieth-century historian 'If the Fenian organisation like other revolutionary secret societies, had its share of corruption and crime, its strength lay not in the evils incidental to it but in its unquenchable idealism'. It was this idealism that enabled Fenianism to survive against such great odds, and eventually achieve, in large measure, its ultimate goal of an independent Ireland.

Photo 48. Two generations of Fenians: John Daly, Thomas Clarke and Seán MacDiarmada.

Photo 49. John Devoy (1842–1928). A native of Kill, Co Kildare, he served in the French Foreign Legion, returning to spearhead IRB infiltration of the British Army. Imprisoned in 1866 and amnestied in 1871, he built the Clan na Gael organisation in America into a powerful and influential body.